D0470868

FENCE STYLE

FENCE STYLE

Surround Yourself
with Charm & Elegance

James Harper & Margie Roe

Sterling Publishing Co., Inc.
New York

Written By: James Harper
Margie Roe
Editor: Mickey Baskett
Design & Illustration: Margie Roe
Photography: Bob Busby
Margie Roe
Mark Roe
Jerry Mucklow
Copy Editing: Sylvia Carroll
Graphics: Dianne Miller, Karen Turpin
Styling: Laney Crisp McClure
Administration: Jim Baskett

Acknowledgements

Special thanks to the Home Depot in Brunswick, Georgia, USA, and
J. C. Strother & Sons, St. Simons Island, Georgia, USA, for assistance
in photographing tools

Plaid Enterprises, Inc., 1649 International Blvd., Norcross, GA, USA
for supplying materials for the decorated fences: Durable Colors™
Outdoor paint; Decorator Products® Glazes, Tools, and Stamps;
Stencil Decor® Stencils.

Every effort has been made to insure that the information presented is accurate. Since we have no control
over physical conditions, individual skills, or chosen tools and products, the publisher disclaims any
liability for injuries, losses, untoward results, or any other damages which may result from the use of the
information in this book. Thoroughly read the instructions for all products used to complete the projects in
this book, paying particular attention to all cautions and warnings shown for that product to ensure their
proper and safe use.
No part of this book may be reproduced for commercial purposes in any form without permission by the
copyright holder. The written instructions and design patterns in this book are intended for the personal
use of the reader and may be reproduced for that purpose only.

Library of Congress Cataloging-in-Publication Data Available

Published by Sterling Publishing Company, Inc.
387 Park Avenue South, New York, N.Y. 10016
Produced by Prolific Impressions, Inc.
160 South Candler St., Decatur, GA 30030
© 2000 by Prolific Impressions, Inc.
Distributed in Canada by Sterling Publishing
c/o Canadian Manda Group, One Atlantic Avenue, Suite 105
Toronto, Ontario, Canada M6K 3E7
Distributed in Great Britain and Europe by Cassell PLC
Wellington House, 125 Strand, London WC2R 0BB, England
Distributed in Australia by Capricorn Link (Australia) Pty. Ltd.
P.O. Box 6651, Baulkham Hills, Business Centre, NSW 2153 Australia

Printed in China
All rights reserved
ISBN 0-8069-3945-1

TABLE OF CONTENTS

Foreword

The authors intend this book to serve as a guide for erecting a sturdy, long-standing fence from a variety of materials–how to choose the fence style that best meets your purpose, how to select the tools and materials, how to survey the land and plot the course of the fence so the completed structure reflects the care and hard work that you have dedicated to this task. Beyond that, we want to provide you with some historical sense of the contributions that fences have made to cultures and civilizations around the globe so that you may apply your own thoughts and creativity to a completed project that lends character to the site it encloses and instills pride in your work.

Introduction

Since the beginning of time, when man first applied sticks with sharpened stones to cultivate land for food and started domesticating animals to work the fields, fences have played a critical role in the advancement of civilization. From primitive stone fences that prevented varmints from destroying vegetable gardens and interlopers from rustling cattle to today's elaborate stone, wood, and metal fencing that express the property owner's style and personality while establishing a perception of privacy or security, the fence has persevered. It has enabled an entire nation to better protect its citizens – the Great Wall of China. It has assured a continuing food supply for millions of people just as the barbed wire fence led to the establishment of the great cattle ranches of the West. It has helped protect our loved ones, corralled valued pets and animals, provided a visual boundary of our property, and it has served as a privacy buffer from environmental forces and other outside influences. Above all, we use the fence today to complete the visual appearance of our home. Often, it's the first thing the visitor notices upon entering the yard, and its visual appearance sets the tone for their perception of the people inside.

The word fence has even had a pervasive and lasting influence on language

usage. Webster's describes fence as "a barrier enclosing or bordering a field, yard, etc., usually made of posts and wire or wood, used to prevent entrance, to confine, or to mark a boundary." Evolving from that simple definition are terms such as "mending fences" which reflects a determination to strengthen a severed relationship; "fence sitting", used to describe one who remains uncommitted, undecided, or unwilling to establish a position on issues; and "to fence with", a tactic used by some to evade confrontation or avoid giving a direct answer.

Regardless of how the term is used, fences have remained a vital element of global culture and lifestyle. Good fences, it is said by some, make

Your creativity often plays a major role in the way fences reflect and even improve the property they enclose.

Through the ages, elaborate designs in metal have been used to reflect the craftsmanship and creativity of the homes and properties they protect.

good neighbors. They can also make good neighborhoods, good homes, good families, and good pets. Since the laying of the first boundary, fences have served to protect our privacy while providing a gateway to welcome new friends. They can be as rustic as a homemade twig fence or as ornate as an antique wrought iron masterpiece; as homey as a classic white picket fence or as commanding as

While privacy and security are often the primary objectives, the functionality of fences can even extend to the protection of the environment.

a hand-crafted brick structure. But whatever material you use, always keep in mind its ultimate purpose. As Robert Frost observed in the poem Mending Wall, "Before I built a wall I'd ask to know...What I was walling in or walling out...And to whom I was like to give offense."

Before you begin

There was a time when little consideration needed to be paid to boundaries, property lines, or to possible future uses and purposes. Today, however, we live in a world of private ownership, building codes, and community guidelines. For all these reasons, you should invest a major effort in the planning process for putting up a fence. Among your responsibilities are the following:

Consider Design

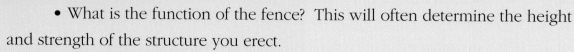

- Your choice of design should work well not only with the property or structure it surrounds but with the environment outside the perimeter of the fence as well.

    - Where is a major activity area? What are the traffic patterns? What view do you want to emphasize or block out? Where will you place the gates and how wide should they be?

- What is the function of the fence? This will often determine the height and strength of the structure you erect.

• Consider the scale of size and the height of the fence in respect to the house or structure it will enclose. Tall fences look better with multi-story homes while a low-slung fence is more compatible with a single-story ranch or cottage style structure.

• Keep in mind the cost and maintenance of a fence when choosing the materials you will use.

• Gauge the effects of sloping property lines when designing the fence.

Building Codes

• Make sure your fence remains within height and setback requirements of the property line.

• Check the property layout or have a survey performed to insure that you are building the fence within the boundaries of your property.

• Check requirements for use of building materials.

• Locate underground utility cables or pipelines before digging post holes.

Neighbors and Property Lines

• It's always best to discuss plans for a fence with your neighbors. Consider with them how their view may be altered by the proposed fence, and

discuss maintenance plans where the fence abuts their property. Above all, make sure your neighbors are aware of the property boundaries.

• Unless you and your neighbor jointly own and share responsibility for the fence (an agreement that is best committed to writing), the structure should be totally within the bounds of your property, including concrete footing.

• The mortgage of your deed or local building departments should include information to help you obtain recorded property line information.

If you are unable to get that information, you can work with your neighbor to establish a workable fence line. If this becomes necessary, you should have that agreement in writing in order to avoid future misunderstandings. If you are unable to reach an agreement on the boundaries, the safest step is to have a surveyor or civil engineer establish the property lines. Consider the Environment

• If you live in an area with many existing fences, consider whether your design will be compatible both with their design and with the site you are enclosing.

• Remember that solid constructed fences don't necessarily block the

wind and rain, they merely redirect it. During a storm, this could pose a greater problem than a fence with gaps or other openings. Louvered and open metal fences, for example, can better redirect the air velocity than a solid wall.

• In colder climates, you must consider the effects of ice, melting snow, etc. Open fences permit the free flow of air and avoid "pooling" from ice or frost that can kill or injure plants.

Consider the Purpose

What do you want your fence to do?

• Serve as a privacy or security barrier.
• Hide utility areas.
• Define a garden or pool area.
• Protect children or pets.
• Provide a buffer from the sun or wind.

Remember, planning is everything when it comes to projects like building a fence. A well-designed, well-built fence can enhance your property values as well as your esteem in the minds of friends and neighbors.

STONE & BRICK FENCES

Stone was the material of choice when man first discovered the need to enclose an area to prohibit the encroachment of pests of both the animal and human variety. Few would argue that it was also the most logical choice–a "no brainer" if you will–for our prehistoric ancestors to choose the material most obviously in abundance.

Yet stone has remained a popular choice for fencing throughout the ages. Certainly, Emperor Qin Shihuangdi of China recognized the enduring protective qualities of natural stone when he elected to construct history's largest and longest "fence"–the Great Wall of China starting in the year 221 B.C. Meandering through mountains and valleys and stretching over 1,500 miles in length, the Great Wall is the longest fortified line ever built, winding through northern China from Lin-yu on the east coast to Kansu province in north-central China. The wall stands about 25 feet high with towers ranging in height to 40 feet and staggered every 200-to-300 yards along the length of the structure. The wall tapers from a width of 25 feet at the base to about 15 feet at the top. Its sides are made of earth, brick and

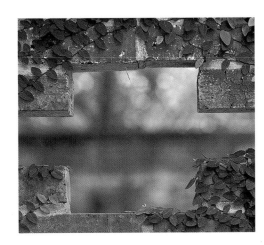

stone, and the top is paved with bricks set in lime where it served as a roadway for horsemen.

The massive wall was centuries in the making with succeeding dynasties conscripting peasants, enemies, and anyone else who was available to work on the structure. Each dynasty added to the height, breadth, length, and elaborated the design, mostly through forced labor. Completed in the 15th Century, the Great Wall stood as a monument to China's greatness and of man's ability to achieve.

Oddly enough, the wall was originally designed to repel unwanted invaders and provide protection for the citizens inside. And while it served well against all forms of physical attack, both the Mongols and the Manchurians were able to take power, not because of a weakness in the

wall but because of corruption and weakness of governments in power that led to poverty and unrest of the people inside. Today, the Great Wall of China is perhaps the world's largest tourist attraction since the Chinese government has eased restrictions against outside visitors and permitted greater mobility on the part of its citizens. Millions of people annually trek to segments of the wall's length to stare in wonder at its historic presence and bask in the panoramic vistas of surrounding mountains, valleys, and streams. Where military leaders once manned the unyielding towers to ward off their enemies, today, hundreds of souvenir shops display a cross-section of handicrafts with craftsmen peddling quilts, porcelain, enamels, hats, and colorful toys to welcome visitors.

The paradox of the
Great Wall, having originated
as a defensive measure only to
fail in its original purpose, is
not alone. In modern times,
we have seen the Maginot Line of concrete and
steel barriers in France that failed to prevent
Hitler's tanks from storming into Paris and
capturing that strategic city during World War II.
Likewise, the much-despised Berlin Wall, in more
recent times, was no match for the relentless
pursuit of freedom when it fell in 1989.

What we have learned from these massive
structures, however, is that stone and masonry
are valued materials in the building of fences
large and small.

BUILDING A STONE FENCE

The stone fence can lend a stately appearance to its surroundings, or it may convey a rustic, almost woodsy look that makes it an ideal companion to English Tudor, bungalow, or cottage style housing. Yet it is versatile enough to complement modern housing as well as original log cabins.

Among advantages of stone are that the fence can be built at practically no cost if the stones are available on property. In addition, the fence can be form fitted into curving or undulating property lines easier than wood or metal fencing. Conversely, building a stone

Stone is easily teamed with wood or metal to create an esthetically pleasing property enclosure.

fence is physically demanding when moving large quantities of heavy materials, and the stone must be properly stacked to assure lasting value.

Traditionally, stone walls are of two varieties - the dry or wet retaining wall. The dry retaining wall, usually under two feet high and constructed without mortar, is dependent on the weight and balance of one stone on top of another to retain stability. Because of the lack of mortar, or bonding material, the dry wall is better used as a retaining wall on sloping property, for decorative effect, or as a garden planter rather than a fully constructed fence line. As noted, the wet retaining wall contains mortar between the stones and is much stronger and more durable. Since the stones are bonded together, they can be stacked higher to form a free-standing

fence. Another approach is to use concrete blocks as the base with stone veneer mortared to the outside of the blocks.

If you choose to build a stone wall, however, you must consider soil conditions. A rainy climate, high water table, or a nearby lake or stream may affect the design of the wall. When soil is wet, its load-bearing capacity is reduced, its weight increases, and it tends to move laterally. In cold climates, wet soil freezes and expands, exerting pressure on the wall. To reduce increased soil pressure, you should install special drainage provisions for all types of retaining walls over two feet high, even dry stone walls. Drainage can be provided by weep holes, gravel backfill, drainage pipe, or a combination of these.

Above: Whether dry wall or mortar, the stone fence provides a stately complement to a variety of architectural styles.

Left: Stone was perhaps the first building material for fences, and it has proven its durability and worth through the centuries.

If you live in a rocky area, you may be able to obtain the appropriate stones free of cost, either on your own property or in nearby fields. For hauling, you'll need a pick-up truck or trailer and you must be careful not to overload. When unloading, deposit the stones as closely as possible to the project site.

In selecting stones, look for those with a solid base, a flat top, and one or more straight, flat sides. For a wall with corners, you'll need a supply of stones with two flat sides that meet at a right angle. Your project will go faster if you use larger stones, but you will tire soon if they are too heavy. Try to limit the stones' weight to under 30 pounds.

Mason's hammer

If you can't locate stones for free, see your local stone yard or quarry. A visit to several sources will enable you to determine what you need at the best price. Prior to delivery, it's best to check the stones to be sure they are the right size and shape for your project.

When working with stone, you'll need heavy-duty gloves, a dust mask, and goggles for protection A spirit level, a mason's hammer, and a wheelbarrow are also needed for stone work. If you are building a wet retaining wall, you will need premixed concrete and a trowel.

BUILDING A STONE FENCE

DRY RETAINING WALL

The dry wall can be quite attractive and is relatively simple to build, using flatter, wider stones whenever possible. To get started, you should first lay stones at least six inches below grade. Where soil conditions are subject to fluctuation, you should dig a trench 12 inches deep and backfill it with a six-inch layer of sand or gravel. If the soil is particularly unstable, a shallow concrete footing may be necessary. Typically, however, sophisticated footing is not required since the stones are not bonded together and will rise and fall from the effects of frost.

The initial, or base layer, should comprise larger stones. Each layer of stone is known as a "course". String a line along the wall as a guide to keep it straight. If you are constructing the wall on a slope, it may require a "batter" or wedge-shaped boards that are flat on one side and

sloping on the other. When driven into the ground, they provide a quick check on inward sloping of the stones. If required, the batter board must remain at right angles to the ground and should be checked with a level. For best results, the stones should be placed as they would lie naturally on the ground. Always lay the stones with the flat side down and fill in spaces with smaller stones. As each level is completed, spread a layer of sandy soil over the top to serve as a kind of mortar. Continue laying courses of stone in the same pattern until you reach the desired height. The top layer of the wall should comprise the flattest and broadest of the stones in order to maximize stability. The planting of ivy or other vines will further assure stability as the roots bind the wall in place over time.

WET RETAINING WALL

While a wet retaining wall requires a greater expertise than the dry wall, especially if you are considering a wall over three feet high, it does lend an air of refinement and permanence to the enclosed area. A mortared wall requires the same care as a dry wall, and you should not rely on the mortar alone for stability. The stones are still held in place by their weight and balance with the mortar acting as bonding agent and filler. Mortared walls also require a substantial concrete footing to prevent excessive settling and cracking, along with a drain system for retaining walls.

Almost any type of stone can be used in a wet wall, but stone with straight sides that can be laid in courses is best to work with. The stones should be laid out ahead of time so they are conveniently reached as the wall progresses.

To begin, pour a concrete footing 12 inches thick and wide enough to extend six inches beyond the wall on both sides.

The footing must be below the frost line and have a six-inch layer of gravel beneath it to prevent the effects of groundswell. For additional stability, place at least two steel rebars horizontally in the footing.

When using mortar, never lay more than three courses, or two feet in height, in a day in order for the mortar to set enough to withstand the weight of the next layer of stone. A standard mortar mixture for stone is one part lime, three parts portland cement, and nine parts sand. Water should be added slowly until the mixture stands in peaks. Don't allow the mortar to touch the face of the stone, or the lime will leave stains. Also, remember to wear gloves when working with mortar and stones which can be very rough on the hands.

In order for the mortar to bond well, the stones must be clean. First, spread a one-inch layer of mortar over the footing at one end and lay a bondstone (a rock wide or long enough to stretch across the width of the wall). Then spread more mortar, lay large stones along the outside edges of the wall, and fill in the center with small stones, rubble, and mortar. Complete each layer in this manner, laying a bondstone every five or six feet. Unless the stones are stable enough to keep the wall vertical, you will need to batter the walls one inch per two feet.

You should keep the completed wall cool and damp for about a week in order to extend the curing time and strengthen the mortar. You can mist the wall with a garden hose and cover it with plastic sheeting. A temporary shading device may even be necessary.

METAL FENCES

While nature's provenance provided stone and wood for fencing materials, it was man's ingenuity that led to the use of metal for fence building.

Why metal? In many instances, there is no other low-cost alternative that compares with the strength, durability and relative lightness of iron. Its open design withstands the intensity of winter winds and snows, and during warmer months it sends a welcome to climbing vines and flowers that add color to the landscape.

History doesn't record where and when the first metal enclosure was attempted, but it most likely occurred in

Great Britain during the Victorian era, the
latter part of the 19th century. The
appearance of elaborately designed cast
iron molds for gates and fences coincided
with the emergence of a strong middle

class society in England during the reign of Queen Victoria. As prosperity spread across the country, many wealthy property owners began to express their newfound worth in terms of architecturally aggressive homes with wide, sweeping porches, steep gables and balconies, often paired with intricate gingerbread trim. To provide an appropriate boundary that reflected the craftsmanship and creativity of the home

The ornate metal fence of cast or wrought iron is often a statement of the prosperity enjoyed by the property owner.

itself, the English property owner soon turned to cast iron for fences that would mirror and even enhance the homesite.

Cast iron, followed shortly by the more malleable wrought iron, offered Victorian homeowners the opportunity to indulge their creative fancy. Replicas of crosses and spearheads adorned early iron gate posts, but a large variety of styles and patterns emerged as the popularity of metal fences grew. Flowering vines and bunches of grapes soon blossomed across broad expanses of iron fences, along with

scrolls, motifs, and family crests common to 18th century lifestyles.

It was not long before their counterparts in America embraced the English trend toward metal fencing. Initially popular in major seaport cities such as Boston, New Orleans, Charleston, SC, and Savannah, GA, the use of metal soon spread to inland cities such as Chicago and Pittsburgh. The widespread impact of hand and machine-crafted metal fences can be seen today in all of those cities and in San Francisco, Washington, DC, Philadelphia and New York where the original grandeur of ornamental ironwork remains a highly prized framework for homes of historic or sentimental value.

The grandeur of ornamental metal fences remains a highly sought framework for homes and buildings with historic or sentimental presence.

If beauty and sophistication were among the attributes that led to the popularity of iron fencing, it was the functionality of another type of metal that sealed its contribution to society. That metal was the common wire fence that made its biggest impact during the settlement of the western United States during the late 1800s. While light gauge steel wire had been used for various agricultural and ranching purposes for many years, it took a new "twist" on that venerable metal to create a volatile and lasting effect on frontier life. That twist came in the form of a barbed coil whose sharply pointed tips were strung across the length of the wire. When stretched between upright wood posts, barbed wire offered a low cost enclosure for truck farmers and ranchers alike.

Invented by a DeKalb, IL farmer, named Joseph F. Glidden in 1874, barbed wire was at first rejected by the big ranchers who opposed fencing in any form, preferring instead the "open range" approach to raising cattle. As vegetable farmers and other homesteaders proliferated, however, it became obvious that even the die-hard open range advocate would have to fence his property to establish legal ownership of ranches that embraced thousands of acres. It was equally apparent that barbed wire was superior to smooth, light gauge wiring because the thorn-like prongs discouraged cattle from charging through it and wandering onto neighboring properties.

Even as progress demanded change, barbed wire was not an easy sell. In Texas, for example, the Legislature threatened to outlaw the use of barbed wire until two extraordinary salesmen -- Henry B. Sanborn and John (Bet-a-Million) Gates were dispatched to San Antonio by Glidden to set up a trial barbed wire corral to demonstrate the effectiveness of the newly fabricated metal. The corral was built on the main plaza of the Alamo City and a small herd

Barbed wire fences helped establish the United States as the world's leading agricultural nation.

of Longhorns were placed inside to convince ranchers that the wire would contain their cattle without harming them in any way.

The San Antonio experiment was so successful that Texas soon became the site of history's largest deployment of barbed wire fencing. Strangely, the burning of the Texas Capitol in Austin was the event that ignited the fencing project. To replace their old building with a new and grander structure, Texans swapped three million acres of Panhandle land to a group of Chicago contractors and financiers for the money to build the new Capitol. The Chicago syndicate, in turn, established on the acreage one of the West's storied ranches, the XIT. The name XIT was said to represent "Ten in Texas" for the ten counties in which the land was located. As shrewd investors, the new XIT owners realized that fencing would be critical to protecting their holdings. They also

recognized quickly the cost advantage of barbed wire over other fence material. By the time the project was complete, some 800 miles of barbed wire was strung across the three million Panhandle acres to make the XIT the biggest ranch in Texas.

Unlike the majestic and enduring cast and wrought iron fences that remain as stalwart testimony to the enduring qualities of metal, the XIT ranch eventually faded from the Texas landscape along with the history-making fence project. Still, barbed wire remains a popular, cost-effective

fence material for farmers and ranchers throughout rural America, and various offshoots of these early-day enclosures are widely used in all parts of the globe today.

The intricate, hand-crafted metal fence of yesteryear has yielded to the more mundane but functional chain-link fence of today.

Working With Metal

While some consider the construction of metal fences to be too difficult even for the handiest of non-professionals, the fact is that many people have completed chain-link and wire mesh enclosures to their satisfaction. Perhaps one reason for the hesitance to tackle a chain-link project is the lack of familiarity with the use of a fence stretcher, one of the required tools for the project. The fence stretcher is not a difficult tool to master, however, and is absolutely necessary to apply the correct tension and assure a taut, long-lasting structure.

The entire project should require only a few days and can be accomplished in two phases -- the setting of the posts followed later by the installation of rails and chain-link material. You may want to enlist the help of a friend in order to further simplify the project.

gloves

trowel

The Basics

With the exception of the fence stretcher, the tools and materials required for chain-link fence building are basic in nature and are easily available from fence suppliers. They include:

- Fence Stretcher--this can be rented from the supplier or other equipment rental sources.

- Post-hole digger--a necesseity for most fence projects, metal or wood, and also easy to rent.

- Concrete and trowel along with container for mixing concrete.

- The usual assortment of gloves, pliers, and an adjustable wrench for light stretching and bending requirements of the project. See pages 54 and 55 for other useful tools you will need.

gas powered auger, optional for digging holes in difficult areas.

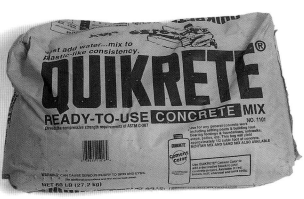

concrete

string level

hammer

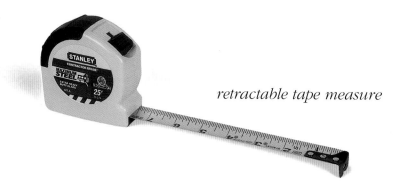

retractable tape measure

level

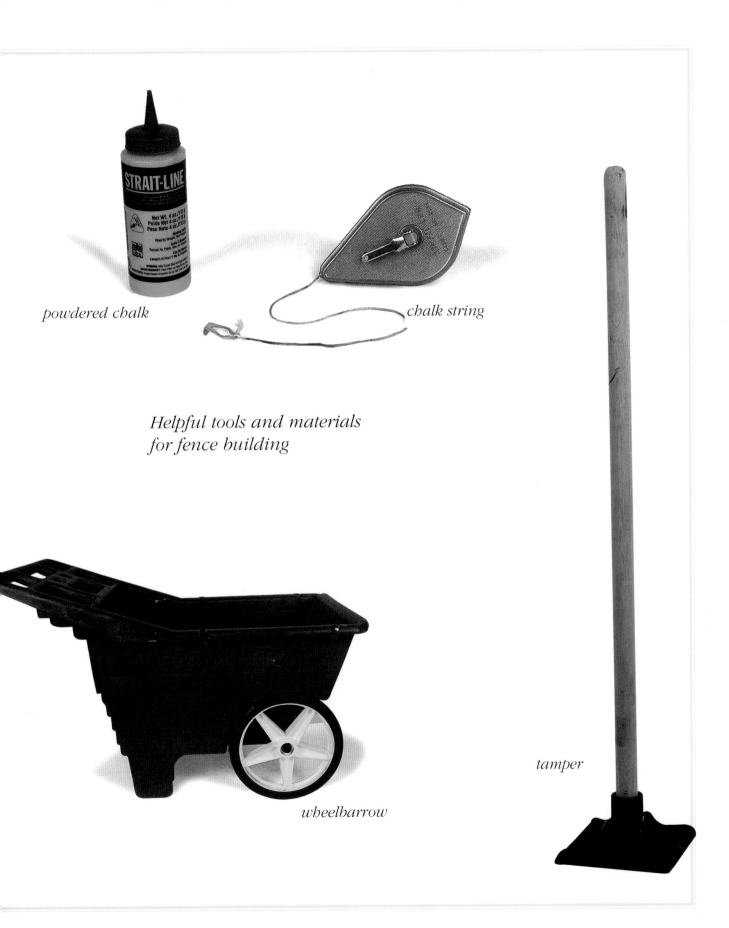

powdered chalk

chalk string

Helpful tools and materials
for fence building

tamper

wheelbarrow

Setting the Posts

As with any fence project, make sure you have adequately surveyed the area to be enclosed and pinpointed the locations for gates, corners, etc.

1. Once you have completed this necessary first step, you are ready to start digging holes for the metal posts. Unless the project covers a wide expanse of property, you'll probably make do with a manual post hole digger, but if you want to speed up this part of the job you may elect to spend more money to rent a digging machine.

The fence posts should be set in concrete no more than 10 feet apart (many suggest that the posts be located from six to 10 feet

circumference of fenced area

placement and swing direction of gates

Scaled drawing of lot and structures

apart). For end posts, those that anchor the corners or serve as gate posts, you should dig holes 12 inches wide and 36 inches deep. Line post holes should be dug eight inches wide and 36 inches deep. Mark the ground line on the post with a crayon before sertting it. The end posts whould be two inches taller than the chain link material, and line posts should be two inches shorter.

2. Once the holes are dug, fill each with concrete and set the post in the hole. Leave about one inch of concrete above ground level. Just before the concrete sets, plumb the posts and adjust the height so the crayola mark you made

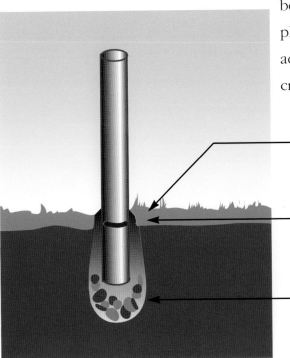

when pouring concrete, leave about one inch of concrete above ground level

line up crayon mark with ground level and make sure post is level.

for end posts, dig holes 12 inches wide and 36 inches deep

earlier is at ground level. Repeat this process with each post, and make sure the gate posts are exactly three feet apart, inside to inside.

3. Again, before the concrete sets, check the height of the line posts by stretching a string between two end posts four inches below the top. If a line post is below the string, raise it even with the string; if below the string, drive the post further into the ground to bring it in line.

4. With the posts all in place and correctly aligned, allow the concrete to dry completely (check drying requirements on label of concrete sacks).

A cautionary note: Do not use quick-drying concrete in setting the posts since you will need time to make necessary adjustments.

Installing the Wire

5. With the posts set firmly in the concrete, it's time to install the top railings. Start by sliding tension bands and brace bands onto the end posts, then add the post caps. Slip the top rail through eye tops, and cut to fit with a hacksaw, then add the rail ends. Bolt the rail to the brace bands.

6. Now that the top rail is in place, you are ready to install the chain-link material. Slip the tension bar of the fence stretcher into

the first row of wire material, and bolt the
bar to the tension bands. Using tie wires,
attach the chain-link fencing loosely to
the rail, then set the stretching bar three
feet from the other end of the wire.
Attach the fence stretcher to the bar and
end post and stretch the chain-link
material. To check the tension of the wire, make sure it is taut but gives easily when pushed.
Remove the extra wire and again insert the tension bar and bolt to tension bands. Again using tie
wires, attach the chain link to the top rail every 24 inches and to the line posts every 12 inches.

Setting the Gates

7. To set the gate, install the bottom post hinge
with the pin pointing up and the the top post hinge with
the pin pointing down. Position the gate with the top
aligned with the top of the fence. Finally, adjust the
hinges and set the gate latch.

Variations

In addition to chain link fencing, wire mesh and ornamental iron are also popular materials for metal fences.

The **wire mesh** fence is very inexpensive and much easier to install than a chain link enclosure. The material is readily available at most hardware stores, lumber yards, or building supply centers. The gridlike and rectilinear weaves of wire mesh are quite attractive while heavier materials have inersections of wire welded at the joint, making a rigid fabric that makes a durable and appealing fence.

The steps for installing wire mesh are quite simple. In most cases, wood posts are used instead of the metal posts of a chain-link fence. Again using a post-hole digger, the wood posts are set in concrete, all at the same height.

The wire mesh then is stretched between the posts, and a wood railings are nailed or screwed to the posts at top and bottom.

Ornamental iron, on the other hand, is a classic fencing material that should be designed and fabricated by a professional. Most of today's ornamental iron work is fabricated with hollow steel tubing in place of wrought iron. This type of fencing is attractive and sophisticated but requires the apprpriate setting to be effective. It conveys a rich, light, and formal appearance and can range in design from a strong, vertical look to a complex variety of twists and turns.

An option for those who wish to construct an iron fence but discover that professional work is beyond their budget is to explore the use of prefabricated products designed for home installation. Prefab material can be found at many home improvement centers and building supply outlets, along with tips on installation.

Wood Fences

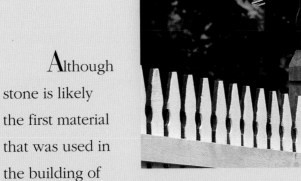

Although stone is likely the first material that was used in the building of a fence, there is no question that the versatility, availability, and sheer attractiveness of wood has made it the leading choice of today's fence builders. Despite deep and appropriate concerns for the protection of old growth and rain forests, the fact remains that wood is a replenishable product, in abundant supply and attractively priced. Add to that the fact that wood is so versatile -- easily cut to specific lengths for a custom-designed project or shaped to reflect the contours of an undulating property line, even stained or painted to complement its surroundings. Considering all these factors, it is ironic that the picket fence, possibly the most notable and charming of wooden enclosures, had its beginning as a military defense measure.

During the historic battles that raged through Europe and England during the 18th and 19th centuries, detachments of soldiers who manned military posts were known as piquets while the word fence at that time was loosely translated to mean defense. The military posts were constructed of high, tightly built wooden enclosures with sharply pointed tips.

Later, during the settlement of

remote areas of the western territory of the United States -- from 1850 through the 1890s -- Army divisions were dispatched to serve as the protectors of early settlers and to safeguard agents of the government and private industry in their efforts to survey the land and establish rail lines and other services in the far west. In order to accomplish their assignment, the frontier soldiers were

required to construct fortresses to serve as their base of operations and to protect homesteaders and government employees from attack by Indians and other renegade forces.

Unfortunately, much of this area extended across barren plains which were virtually devoid of trees and large natural stone that could have been used to construct secure western outposts. Instead, military forces ranged far and wide to scrounge saplings from trees whose growth was stunted by lack of water and constantly swirling winds. Combinations of dwarf cedar, mesquite,

or pine limbs of sufficient length were pieced together to form the basic requirements for a protective wall.

Following the lead of their British counterparts, the soldiers sharpened the trees into spear-like stakes with points at either end. They dug a narrow trench, drove the posts into the ground, then backfilled the trench to create a firm foundation for the posts. Using the longest of the tree trunks, the workers then added railings at the top and bottom of the fence line for stability. While the completed wall was no match for stone walls or wooden barriers built from

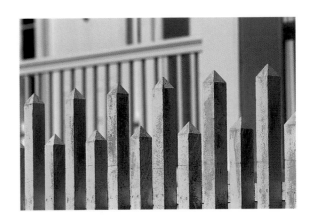

mature tree trunks, the sharpened tips were enough to discourage attackers from climbing the walls, and armed guards were strategically placed along the top of the barrier to prevent the enemy from storming through the gate. These walls of native trees served as the perimeter of many frontier outposts, and the concept for using sharply pointed tips to discourage outsiders from scaling walls of defense gained in popularity.

Homesteaders and other early western settlers, like the soldiers, saw the wisdom of using sharpened stakes

Above: When a fence is developed with a purpose in mind, the result is not just a barrier but an enduring statement of the property owner's values and concerns.

Right: While privacy and security are often the primary objectives, the functionality of fences can even extend to the protection of the environment.

Fences have played a critical role in civilization's progress, starting with the first crude stone fences that protected crops and field animals to today's stylized enclosures that often serve to enhance property values.

to bar entrance to their property and adapted the design when building fences to protect their vegetable gardens. While property owners could easily admit welcome guests, the sharpened stakes, or piquets, prevented others from climbing the fence to raid the vegetable gardens. Thus was born the idea for a wooden picket fence that has come to symbolize warmth and charm rather than a barrier against interlopers.

Working with Wood

While all fence materials present the builder with an opportunity to achieve a certain "look" that enhances the site to be enclosed, none can compete with wood for the variety of available options. The homeowner may select from different types of wood, a variety of pre- or custom-cut styles, natural or stained colors, woods of various length and width, patterned

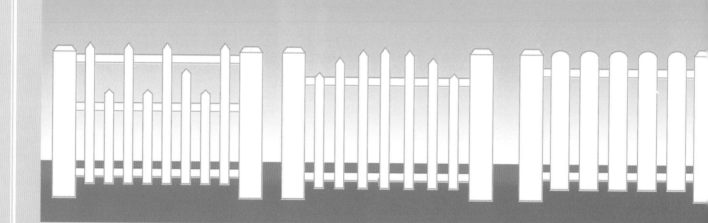

woods, or even pre-cut and shaped panels. The wood fence can
be open and inviting, high and tightly enclosed for privacy, plain
and sturdy, or elaborately designed and finished. The options are
so broad in scope that the homeowner would be wise to research
the fence project thoroughly before digging the first posthole.
With that in mind, following are a few considerations.

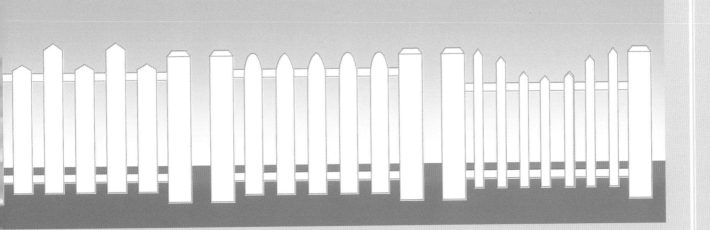

Designs in Wood

As noted earlier, wood fence designs are virtually without limit. Most, however, will require the same basic framework of posts and rails as detailed previously, although spacing between the posts may vary according to design. Among the more popular wood fence designs are the following:

Classic Picket

This classic design fits almost any setting, both formal and informal. Among its advantages, the picket fence contains children and pets without obstructing views.

With the posts in place, cut them about six inches shorter than the fence height. Nail the top rail to the tops of the posts and the bottom rail between the posts, about six inches above ground level. Pickets can be ordered precut. If you cut your own, make simple pointed stakes with a circular saw or use a jigsaw for more elaborately shaped tops. Stretch and level a string across the bottom of the posts for aligning the pickets. For spacing, you can use a spare picket for even placement.

Vertical Board

Among the most popular of wood fence styles, vertical boards offer a great deal of flexibility. They can be arranged in various patterns, either butted tightly together, spaced like slates, set in a slanted angle like louvers, or nailed on both sides of the framing in staggered fashion. Any size of dimension lumber can be used, although the larger sizes are stronger, more economical, and easier to install.

The most common construction is to use 4x4 posts set eight feet apart. A top rail is set on top of the post, and a bottom rail is installed between posts. The fencing boards

are then nailed to one side of the framing or the other. In some cases, they are nailed on both sides, or even installed between the rails.

Stacked Rails

This design eliminates traditional wood posts entirely. Rails can be 4x4s, 6x6s, or any other dimensioned, large-scale timbers. They are stacked on top of each other and either spiked together or threaded onto vertical pipes or rebar (in place of wood posts). Rows are staggered for stability. For even more stability, you may pour a concrete foundation on which to set the bottom rails. The rails are attached to each other by threading them over pipes set into the concrete or by nailing each rail into the one below it with 12-inch spikes. The length of the rails can vary.

Post-and-Rail (Board)

For the basic post-and-rail fence, the rails are placed between the posts before the concrete is entirely set. You will first need to cut holes through the posts and shape the rails to fit. After setting the end post into the post-hole, place the line post in the hole and , while tilting it, insert the other end of the rail. Check the plumb of the post, tamp down the earth fill, and repeat the process at the next post.

For the post-and-board fence, cut 1x4 or 1x6 boards to fit between posts. Measure from centers of the line posts, and add the full width of end posts. Attach top row of boards with nails and check with a level. Use a spacer to align middle and bottom rows of boards.

Varieties of Fences

To this point, we have discussed the most popular types of fences, using the most commonly available materials. Obviously, however, there are many other approaches to fence building that remain popular and involve non-classic choices in both design and materials. Some of these approaches include:

Slats

Similar to pickets but taller, slats present a simple, crisp look and clean lines. The height of the fence and the relatively small scale of the slats give the fence a look of refinement. Slats can be purchased by the piece or by the bundle at lumber yards. The cost is moderate, but it takes time to assemble and construct a slat fence.

Lattice

A classic style for garden fences, the criss-cross pattern of lattice creates a formal design that invites the growth of foliage for a light and lively effect. Lattice offers great flexibility in design, allowing the builder to vary spacing between members to achieve a custom look and feel. Prefabricated sheets of lattice are available from lumber yards, and it's quick and easy to install.

Basket Weave

As the name implies, basket weave siding is woven together. These fences look best if undulation is minimized, and this is accomplished by using one thin spacer for each bay (distance between posts). Basket weaves are best used to enclose large areas, and they are fairly easy to install. Very thin materials look best and are surprisingly strong and inexpensive. Basket weave materials are available at lumber yards.

Stakes

Stakes make a sturdy, attractive fence. The rich surface texture of stakes easily harmonizes with the landscape and gardens. Because they are split, stakes have a rough finish, but the finished look is one of refinement and informality. Stakes are sold by the piece or by the bundle at lumber yards, and construction time is not extensive.

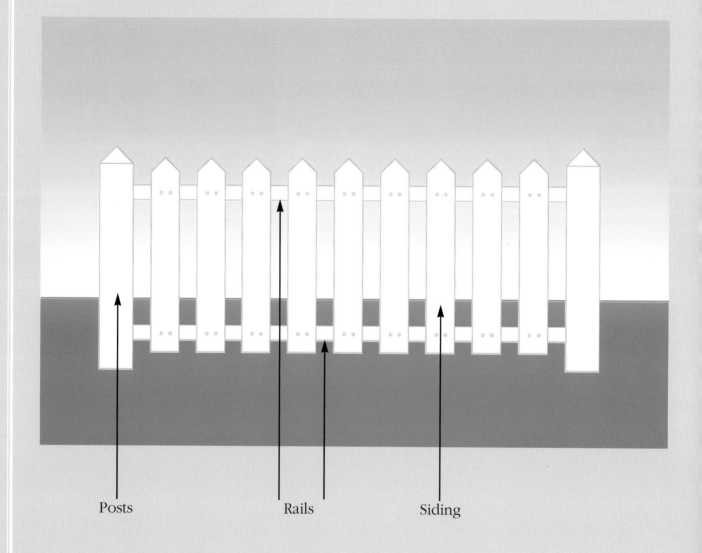

Posts   Rails   Siding

Taming the Slope

There are several approaches to locating sections of the fence along a sloped area. First, you will need to determine the rise and run of the slope by driving a short stake at the top of the slope and a long stake at the bottom. The longer stake should be higher than the bottom of the short stake. Tie a string to the stakes, attach a line level, and adjust the string until it is level.

Using the rise and run measurement, you can determine on paper if you prefer to follow the slope by keeping rails parallel to the slope -- as you would in building a post-and-rail fence. For an uneven slope, you may choose a stepped fence. In this structure, post heights and intervals between posts may differ. Fence panels are cut to fit the slope, and the bottom rail is parallel to the slope.

Using wood, it's important that you consider the overall fence design and how it will impact the landscape. In other words, determine what style best fits your house and neighboring properties. If slopes are involved, you must be prepared to adjust your material requirements. Equally important, make sure there are no gas, water, or power lines below ground where you plan to dig post holes, and be prepared to reposition the posts if any of these exist.

Know Your Wood

For fence building you will likely be using softwood. The term softwood means that the wood comes from a cone-bearing tree and has no bearing on its strength. Your choices of decay-resistant types of wood include redwood, cedar, pine and cypress. A practical option is pressure treated wood which contains chemical preservatives that guard against rot. For layout batterboards and temporary braces, you may need different sizes of untreated lumber in 2x2, 1x4, 2x4, or 2x6 sizes, depending on the scope of the project.

Always remember, when working with treated wood you should wear goggles, gloves, long sleeves, and pants, along with a dust mask. You should wash any areas of your skin that comes in contact with sawdust, and you should launder separately any of your clothes that are exposed to sawdust from treated lumber. Always bury or bag wood scraps; do not burn them.

Lumber Grades

Dimensional lumber (2 to 4 inches thick)

No. 1 (construction)	Few defects; no knots larger than $1\text{-}1/2$ inches, no checks, splits, or warps
No. 2 (standard)	More defects than No. 1; may have knots larger than 2 inches or checks, no splits or warps
No. 3 (utility studs)	More defects than No. 2; may have checks, splits, or warps
Joists and planks	Free of defects that affect strength or rigidity

Boards (less than 2 inches thick)

Select B and BTR	Highest quality, virtually free of defects or blemishes; expensive and not always available
Select C (choice)	High quality; few defects or blemishes
Select D (quality)	Quality; some defects and blemishes
No. 1 common (colonial)	Small, minor defects and blemishes; limited size ranges and not always available
No. 2 common (sterling)	More defects and blemishes than No. 1 common; may have knots of up to 4 inches
No. 3 common (standard)	Larger, coarser defects and blemishes than No. 2 common; may have small knotholes
No. 4 common (utility)	Larger, coarser defects and blemishes than No. 3 common; may have larger knotholes

Dimensional lumber (2 to 4 inches thick)

No. 1 (construction)	Few defects; no knots larger than $1\frac{1}{2}$ inches, no checks, splits, or warps
No. 2 (standard)	More defects than No. 1; may have knots larger than 2 inches or checks, no splits or warps
No. 3 (utility studs)	More defects than No. 2; may have checks, splits, or warps
Joists and planks	Free of defects that affect strength or rigidity

tape measure

At minimum, you'll need heavy-duty gloves, wheelbarrow, stakes for locating posts, heavy-duty hammer or mallet, sledge hammer, post-hole digger (can be rented), garden spade and sharpshooter shovel, tape measure, mason's line, plumb bob, bottled chalk-line powder, or fluorescent layout paint, gravel for backfill,

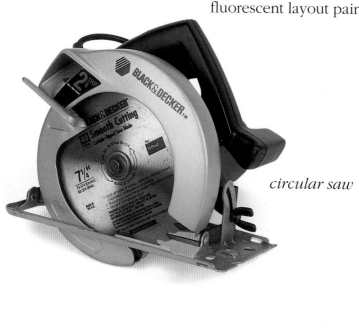

circular saw

plumb bob

pre-mixed concrete, a trowel and galvanized nails.

Specialized tools that may be best to rent or borrow include the following:

- Power Auger for drilling holes in rocky ground, or post hole digger
- Six-foot rock bar to remove larger stones.
- Circular saw, saber saw, power miter saw (or hacksaw with miter box).
- Wood chisel.
- Cordless drill.

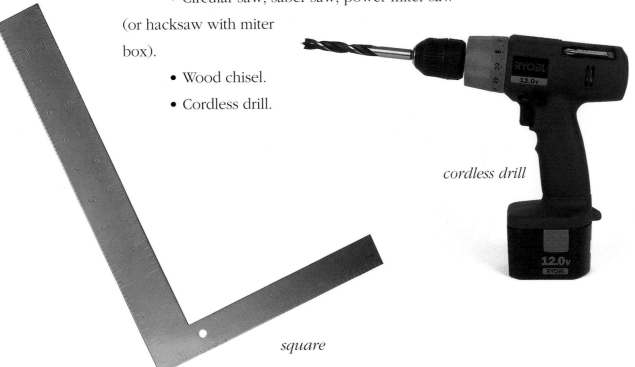

cordless drill

square

string level

metal clamp

power auger

adjustable wrench

hammer

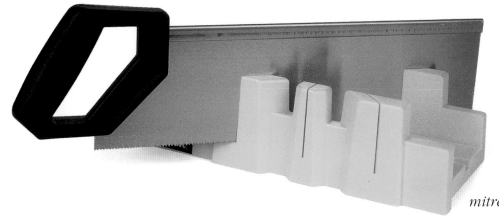

mitre box

jigsaw

Setting Fence Posts

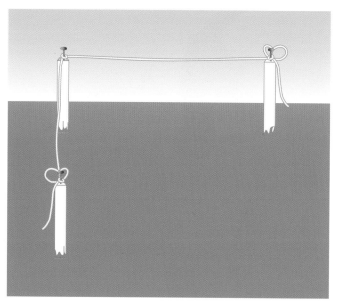

It's best to use pressure-treated 4x4 or 6x6 lumber for end posts and gate posts. Line posts can be 4x4 if the fence is under four feet high and 6x6 or larger for taller fences. Set the posts no more than eight feet apart. You will also need to allow for a gate. The following steps are recommended:

1. To locate the posts, drive stakes into the ground where the end posts will be. Attach a string to both stakes, keeping the string above the grass and making sure it remains taut. To position the line posts, measure the distance with steel tape, and drive stakes into the ground at the appropriate spots.

2. Using the post-hole digger or power auger, create holes for the posts, making them slightly wider than the post and increasing the width at bottom. Make the holes deep enough for at least 20 inches of the post's length if the post is less than six feet, or 30 inches for a post six feet or longer. Add an extra six inches to make room for gravel. In clay soil or for concrete, increase the hole's width to two to three times the post's diameter.

3. Shovel five to six inches of gravel into the bottom of each hole, or place a large flat

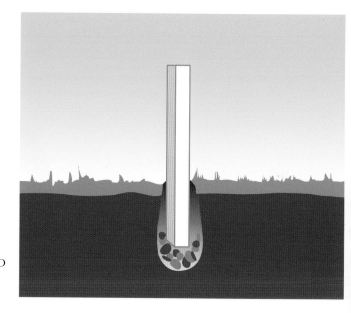

rock inside each hole before adding gravel. In addition to providing drainage, this will prevent decay, especially in posts that are set in concrete collars where it's important to keep the ends out of the concrete.

4. To brace the end post, drive two stakes into soil at adjacent sides of the post. Attach a 1x2 board to each stake with one nail. Set the post in the hole and check plumb with a level on the fact of the post. Then nail the brace to the post. Plumb the adjacent face, and nail the brace. To check the height and plumb of the line posts, hang a line level on two strings extended between the end posts at the top and bottom.

5. Place two to three inches of gravel in the post hole. Shovel four-inch layers of soil on top, tamping each layer down with a 2x4, and repeat until soil is overflowing above ground level. Mold the soil, sloping from the post down to the ground. If you use concrete instead of soil, allow the concrete to overflow the hole. Using a trowel, slope the concrete away from the post. Check plumb of the post. Let concrete set (see instructions for drying time) before

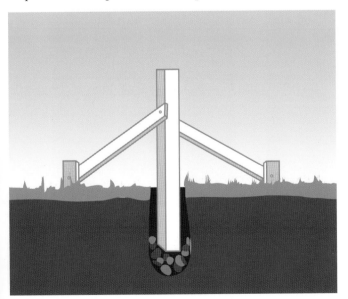

removing the braces. Fill gaps with a flexible urethane sealer.

6. If frost heaving is a problem, after setting the post in the bottom layer of gravel, fill the hole with subsoil to within six inches of the top and use a 2x4 to tamp it down. Force large stones around the post, then fill the hole with topsoil, mounding it up around the post. In sandy soil or in places where the water level is high, use concrete instead of soil and rocks.

Rails & Siding

With the concrete set and the posts in place, you are ready to add rails and siding. By this time, you have determined which style of fence to build, and that will determine your next step.

Basically, the framework for your fence is complete and you can purchase precut rails and siding for final assembly. Treat freshly cut wood and areas that will touch the cuts with a wood preservative. Before assembling the fence, coat each piece of lumber with a water-repellent sealer, stain, or paint.

In attaching the rails to the posts, you may use lap, butt, rabbet, and mortise-and-tenon joints. There are several approaches you can take to attach the rails, including the following:

a. Cut so the top rails are flush with the tops of the boards.

b. Cut so the posts are 6 to 12 inches shorter than the finished height of the fence and the boards extend above the top rails.

c. Cut so that the tops are higher than the boards and either bevel the post tops or

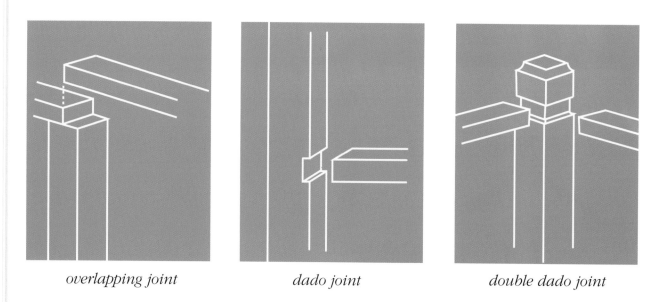

overlapping joint   *dado joint*   *double dado joint*

attach cap rails. Attach the top rails first. Usually, they are set on top of the posts and facenailed with two 16d nails at each post. Use 2x4s long enough to span two or three bays (distance between posts), and locate all of the joints over the posts.

d. Cut the bottom rails to fit between the posts. There are several ways to attach them. The strongest is with metal fence clips that are nailed to the posts. These can be angles that go below the rails, or have pockets that the rails slip into. You can also toenail the ends of the rails into the posts, using 8d nails and predrilling the holes to prevent splitting. Use dado or mortise-and-tenon joints for a more crafted look.

e. Check to be sure they are square before fastening the rails securely to the posts with galvanized nails. For a clean, finished look, sink the nails slightly and cover with putty.

f. If you should select heavy siding for the finished project, you'll need to add a middle rail. Since the boards will eventually shrink, you may want to use tongue-and-groove boards or hide the gaps with battens.

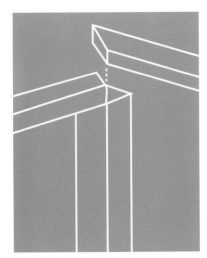

bias miter joint

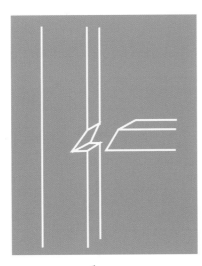

angle groove

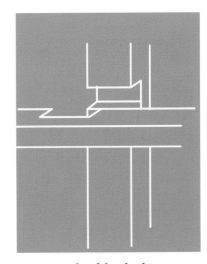

double dado

Gates

Gates may be designed to complement or contrast with the fence. Because the opening and closing of gates can place stress on the posts, the posts should be firmly set. When measuring space between posts for the size of the gate, allow room for hinges and latches.

1. Assemble the gate frame face down, driving galvanized nails into lap joints. Cut the brace to butt against the rails and run it from bottom hinge corner to the opposite corner. Make sure the frame is square, using an L-square.

2. Next, nail two outer pickets or boards flush with the gate frame, making sure they will be level with the fence pickets. Space the remaining pickets or boards evenly between them, keeping a level line across the top.

3. Then, attach one leaf of hinges to the gate rails. Set the gate in place and support with wood blocks on the sides and bottom while securing the other leaf of hinges to the gate post and attaching the latch. To support a large gate, make a cross brace from 2x4 lumber and miter the ends to fit the frame. Use a half-lap joint where the two pieces cross. For support, add glue and screws.

Repairs

All wood fences eventually will need repairs. Some common treatments include the following:

• To steady a wobbly, decay-free post, drive pressure-treated wood wedges into the ground around the post, wrap it with wire, or use a two-piece metal sleeve, drive it into the ground, and nail it to the post.

• To steady a post with decay underground, sink a new, shorter post next to it in concrete and bolt them together with carriage bolts. Saw through the old post two inches above the soil line and remove the decayed wood.

• If a 6x6 post is rotted above ground, saw the top part of the post off below the damaged area. Make a new section from pressure-treated wood and join it to the old post with a half-lap joint and carriage bolts.

• For ground-level rot in a post set in concrete, chisel away the decayed wood below soil (you may have to chisel away part of the concrete as well) and drive three large nails halfway into each side of the post. Then make a plywood form to surround old footing and coat its insides with motor oil. Mix concrete and fill the form. Tamp concrete down, then slope it. When concrete is set, remove the form.

• To replace part of a rotted or splintered rail, cut out the damaged area. Splice in a new piece made from pressure-treated wood. Glue, screw, or bolt the pieces together. If you use glue, apply C-clamps to hold together until glue dries.

• To replace a rail, saw off the old one as close to the post as possible, then cut a new piece to the exact length required. Join the new length to posts with angle irons at each end, then caulk with sealing compound.

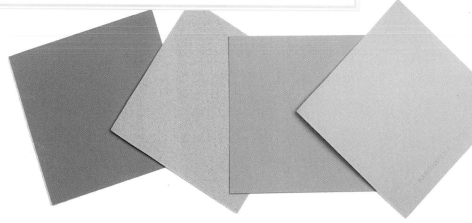

To apply the final touch that gives your fence its distinctive character, you may choose from a variety of finishes ranging from clear water repellents to paints, bleaches and stains. Here are some options:

•Paints:
While they require more work to apply than other finishes, need more maintenance, and are costly, paints create solid color effects and permit the use of lower grades of lumber in the fence since their opaque quality conceals defects in the wood. Paint is best used on smooth-finished wood surfaces where it's easy to apply. There are two broad categories of paint--exterior alkyds which are oil-based (more durable and costlier); and exterior latex which are water-based (less expensive but less durable).

•Clear-water repellents:

While these provide the least protection for the wood, clear-water repellents are best to retain the wood's natural finish. Repellents add no color to the wood and do not hide wood grain, but they do offer protection from moisture-related weathering. Some products combine a water repellent and wood preservative which offers greater protection from

UV sun rays than a simple wood finish. These finishes must be reapplied every six months to two years.

•Bleaching oils and stains: Sometimes called weathering stains, these applications shorten the time required for wood to take on a weathered appearance. At the same time, they offer greater protection than water repellents. They're frequently used with cedar and when first applied they turn the wood gray. You will need to apply a water repellent every two or three years to assure that the fence is protected from moisture.

•Stains: Somewhat like thin paint, stains add color and a protective coating to the wood and work best on rough lumber. They resist mildew and decay and repel water. Available in a variety of colors, stains can be semi-transparent or opaque. Rather than forming a film over the wood as does paint, stains penetrate the wood to reveal its texture. Stains are available in oil and water-based types. Oil-based stains generally penetrate better, but water-based stains offer more protection from changes in temperature or moisture level. Depending on the wood and weather conditions, stains must be reapplied every few years.

decorating fences

Fences are the perfect blank canvas for all sorts of decorating projects. Fences can be used to hang garden tools; fences can be used much like interior walls in your home are used — to hang shelves for storage of garden implements, to hang garden art, to hang signs; fences can be used as a surface for painting a lovely mural or a flower garden scene.

"As much fun as child's play," you will think to yourself when you begin a fence painting project. Tom Sawyer will have nothing over you when you use one of these fence painting projects in this chapter.

The fences in this section of the book aren't the typical white-washed picket fence. Here we have let imaginations soar with ideas for painting murals, vines, rainbows, and flowers on ordinary wooden fences. Nothing will brighten your space more than these handpainted designs. They are especially nice for giving new life to fences that have become shabby and dull.

Whether you wish to paint some retro flowers, a gentle flowering vine, or a bright rainbow - your fence will echo your creativity and fanciful nature. And the instructions for the individual fence paintings will tell you how - with detailed materials lists, step by step design painting instructions and with patterns you can use to help you place or trace your design onto your fence.

Fences are made to be painted. So let your painted fence make a statement about your joy.

Love of Lilacs

STENCILED & STAMPED DESIGN

by Kathi Malarchuk Bailey

*F*ences *have often been thought of as devices for marking property boundaries or creating barriers for animals. But they have so many more uses, especially when they are decorative. For instance, use a fence to separate a woodsy or serene garden area of your yard from a functional driveway/parking area that leads to an open view of the street. No urban traffic will distract your eye from the lovely natural surroundings.*

This natural cedar fence takes on an air of elegance when graced with a simple stenciled wrought iron pattern and a stamped vining lilac. The cedar fence was left unpainted so that just the lovely floral design adds the color. This is so easy to do - you will be done in time to make lemonade for an afternoon break.

MATERIALS

Fence:
Cedar fence, 6 ft. high
Outdoor Paint :
Medium green
Medium blue
Off-white
Pastel green
Red-violet
Brushes:
Stencil brushes, 3/4" is a good standard size
Flat artist's brush
Other Supplies:
Pre-cut stencil of wrought iron design with leaves
  border design (available at craft stores)
Lilac foam stamp or block print design (available at
  craft stores)
Paper palette (available at craft stores, or use
  disposable plate)
Masking tape
Tape measure
Charcoal pencil

INSTRUCTIONS

1. Measure and mark a horizontal line 15" down from top of fence using a charcoal pencil or soft lead pencil. This line will be used as a measure for placing the wrought iron design. If your fence is shorter or taller, you can decide at what height you will want to place your design.

2. Place the top of the stencil design against the marked pencil line. Stencil the wrought iron design border, stenciling the "wrought iron" areas with medium blue and the leaves with medium green. Reverse the stencil and repeat a mirror image of the pattern directly underneath. Let dry.

3. Measure and mark a horizontal line 8" up from bottom of fence, or at a height you desire. This will be the placement for the wrought iron design at bottom.

4. Repeat the stencil design as in step 2.

5. Measure and mask off with masking tape, a 1/2" horizontal band across fence between the two lower stencils. Paint between tapes with red-violet. Let dry and remove tape.

6. Use the foam stamp or block printing design to add the lilacs. Use the flat artist brush to load light green and medium green onto the foam lilac leaves stamp or block. Refer to photo of project for placement. Block print leaves on fence. Use the photo as a guide for placement. The flowers are placed as if they are peeking through the wrought iron fence. Load flowers block with red-violet, medium blue and off-white all at one time. Block print flowers, referring to photo for placement. Let dry. ❏

Summer Vines & Dragonflies
STENCILED & STAMPED DESIGN

Designed by Kathi Malarchuk Bailey

*Y*ou really need that utility shed at the back of your yard to organize and house your lawnmower and yard/gardening tools. But you hate looking at it. The solution is easy. Simply put a fence in front of it. Not just any fence, mind you, but a fence you have enhanced with lovely painted summer vines and magnolia blossoms. It's easy to create, whether you stencil them or just paint them.

MATERIALS

Fence:
Cedar Fence, 6 ft. high
Outdoor Paint:
Brown
Dark green
Light green
Off-white
Brushes:
Stencil brushes
Flat artist's brush
Other Supplies:
Stencil of summer vine design (available at craft stores)
Foam design stamps of dragonfly and flower blossom - a magnolia was used here (available at craft stores)
Paper palette (available at craft stores, or use disposable plate)

INSTRUCTIONS

1. Stencil vines in random patterns across fence, using light green shaded with dark green.

2. Load flower blossom stamp with off-white - add a little dark green for shading, using the flat artist brush to load the stamp. Refer to photo for color placement on stamp. Stamp flowers randomly among vines as shown in photo.

3. Load dragonfly stamp with brown on the body section of the stamp, off-white on the wings with some dark green shading. Refer to photo for color placement. Stamp dragonflies randomly across fence around vines and blossoms. ❏

Fence Plants

Fences are the perfect foil for plants. Fences welcome vining plants, fences are the perfect backdrop for a row of perennials, and fences also can accommodate hanging pots. These photos show two ways plants adorn fences.

METAL POT HOLDER

Here an element from an elegant past is used to add a bit of style to a rustic wooden fence. This wonderful pot hanger is made from a piece of iron fencing. A decorative element of the iron fence is separated from the rest of the fence and then a metal ring is soldered to the piece to hold a clay pot. The rust only adds to the charm of this piece.

SPONGED CLAY POT
(Photo at top right)

This sponge-painted clay pot holding a delightful English ivy topiary sits upon a stone fence, adding a bit of softness to the fence. The sponging is easy to do. **You will need:** a sea sponge, 4-5 disposable picnic plates, three colors of outdoor paint - dark green, medium green, and white, as well as glazing medium. In each plate place about a quarter-size puddle of paint. Add a few sprinkles of clear glazing medium and mix. Wet the sea sponge and squeeze out the water, you want the sponge slightly damp but not wet. "Pounce" the sponge into the dark green paint and then dab it onto a clean plate to remove excess paint. "Pounce" the sponge onto the pot. Sponge entire pot with this color, allowing some of the pot color to show through. Reload sponge when necessary. Don't overwork the sponging — you want the sponging texture to show clearly. Next, repeat the process with the medium green, allowing some of the dark green to show. Repeat with the white paint. It is as easy as that. Remember to keep a light hand when sponging so sponge texture and all colors can be seen.

A Fence of Art

This picket fence acts as one of the walls for an outdoor garden room. It not only separates the area but it acts as a wall for hanging favorite elements such as antique metal signs, rusted iron decorative brackets, charming birdhouses, and even pots of plants.

Country Garden

OUTDOOR SCREEN

by Anne McCloskey

*H*aving an outdoor cookout? Separate the utilities of cooking and serving from the eating area with this screen. Want to have a garden afternoon tea, but you don't have as many flowers in bloom as you would like? Set up this screen in your garden area for an array of flowers and some privacy, too. The extra beauty of this fence — an outdoor folding screen — is that it's portable! You can reposition it as needed, or use it for some occasions and take it down for others. The canvas panel screen is easy to make with these instructions, and canvas provides the perfect painting surface.

MATERIALS

Outdoor Screen:
Roll of canvas
Six wooden stretcher bars, 14"
Six wooden stretcher bars, 48"
Canvas grippers
Ten metal hinges, 2-1/2"
Staple gun and staples
Phillips head screwdriver
Hand drill
Scissors
Gesso

Acrylic Paints:
Apple green
Bright medium green
Bright pink
Burnt orange
Burnt umber
Forest green
Fuchsia
Gold (yellow-orange)
Jade green
Light blue
Lilac
Medium blue
Purple
Terra-cotta
Ultramarine blue
White
Yellow

Brushes:
Flat — size 2"
Filbert — size 1/2"
Foam brush — size 1"
Small sea sponge

Other Supplies:
Stencil-cutting supplies (stencil material, craft or utility knife, glass or self-healing cutting board)
Black wide tip permanent marker
Paper palette (available at craft stores, or use disposable plates)
Measuring tape
Pencil
Cardboard
Measuring tape
Gloss outdoor varnish

MAKE SCREEN

1. Fit together two 48" stretcher bars (sides) and two 14" stretcher bars (top and bottom) to create panel frame of screen. Repeat for two more panels. Cut three canvas pieces at least 3" larger on all sides than the 14" x 48" frames. Lay one frame on the underside of one canvas piece. With the grippers, pull the canvas very tightly around the stretcher bar at center of one side and secure with a staple. Repeat on opposite side. Repeat on top, then on bottom. Continue pulling and stapling from one side to the other until you have stapled all four sides except for the corners. Neatly tuck and trim all corners, then staple in place. Trim excess canvas.

2. Coat the canvas of each panel with gesso, using a foam brush.

PAINT DESIGN

1. **Sketch Hillside:** Each panel is designed to be a little different from the others; however, the painting should fit together as a scene. Lay the three panels together and lightly sketch a curved line across all three panels to represent a hillside. The line should be approximately one-third of the height down from top of screen. Refer to photo of project.

Instructions continued on page 110

2. **Sky:** Paint the sky across all three panels and down to the curved line of the hill with light blue, using a foam brush.

3. **Clouds:** Create clouds by smearing white paint with a circular motion until it resembles a cloud shape. With a large dry brush, keep swirling softly until it looks light and puffy. Continue the clouds across all panels.

4. **Ground:** Paint from the hill line to the bottom of panels with forest green for a background color. Let dry.

5. **Grass:** Paint lines resembling grass blades with bright medium green, using the filbert brush. Cover the entire forest green area with grass blades. Cross over some of the grass with apple green grass blades to create various shades of green.

6. **Fence:** Using patterns, cut a stencil for one fence post and one horizontal rail. Place the stencil of post at varying angles and sponge with a small amount of white paint. Refer to photo of project for positioning. Stencil four fence posts on each panel. Place the horizontal rail stencil between posts and stencil with white in the same manner as shown in photo. Put fence post stencil back in place and sponge the left side of each with burnt umber. Repeat at tops of the horizontal rails. Touch up any areas that did not sponge well with the filbert brush. Let everything dry.

7. **Tiger Lilies:** Transfer patterns of tiger lilies in place, referring to photo of project. Basecoat all with burnt orange, using the filbert brush. Stroke over the burnt orange with double loaded yellow and burnt orange, using the flat brush. Lightly stroke on terra-cotta around some of the petals to create dimension. Let dry. Draw a light line down the center of each petal and make dots all over each petal with the permanent marker. Draw stamens with the permanent marker and outline them with apple green. As you finish these flowers, line up the panels to make sure there is a continuity to the design, that it continues across the panels. Let dry.

8. **Zinnias:** Refer to photo of project for placement of zinnias. Paint some with shades of pink — double load fuchsia and white on the flat brush and stroke in each petal to form an outer row. Lighten fuchsia with white. Double load the mix with white, and paint an inner row. Create two or three rows of petals. Paint the peach zinnias in the same manner, using terra-cotta and yellow; add white as needed to lighten. Dot the centers with yellow and accent with apple green.

9. **Daisies:** Scatter these about the panels, referring to photo of project. Paint petals with double loaded yellow and white, using the filbert brush. Stroke from outside of petal into the center, one petal at a time.

Lightly stroke burnt orange on some of the petals. Dot centers with apple green. Add black dots. Let dry before drawing in next flowers.

10. **Coneflowers:** Refer to photo for placement. These have distinctive black centers. Create these in the same manner as the daisies. Stroke in the bright pink and white petals with the filbert brush. Paint a large ball in the center with burnt umber and dot around it with the marker. Let dry.

11. **Dephiniums:** Transfer pattern, scattering these around the other flowers (refer to photo for placement). For the blue flowers, double load medium blue and white on the flat brush. Dab on a spiked shape flower within the transferred shape. Paint it lighter at the top and use darker shades of blue at the bottom. Shade the side by dabbing on ultramarine blue; highlight with white. Accent with a hint of lilac. Paint the purple flowers in the same manner, using lilac and white together, then adding purple accents. If color is too strong, tone it down with white. You may also touch the purple flowers with blue accents.

12. **Phlox:** Above the main flowers is a field of smaller purple phlox. Create by dabbing on purple splotches with the flat brush and accenting with lilac.

13. **Violets:** Scatter these around all the flowers. Double load brush with lilac and white and stroke petals into the center in a circle. Dot the center with yellow.

14. **Queen Ann's Lace:** Using a small piece of sea sponge, sponge on white lightly to resemble clusters that grow up to the fence.

15. **Vines and Leaves:** Paint vines that wind around the fence with apple green and bright medium green curved lines. Paint leaves with long strokes of apple green and jade green, using the filbert brush.

16. Soften the fence by adding long strokes of grasses painted with watered down forest green.

17. **Butterflies:** Transfer the larger butterfly pattern to the left panel and the smaller one on middle panel, both in the sky area. Turn the two butterflies at different angles (see photo). Paint butterflies with colors indicated on the patterns. Let everything dry.

FINISH

1. If you need to touch of up the sides of the screen, sponge on white on any areas that have been smudged by paint. Let dry.

2. Liberally apply one or two coats of gloss outdoor varnish to the surface of each panel. Let dry.

3. Measure and mark panel sides where hinges will go. There will be five hinges on each side of middle panel (ten total). Measure to be sure the panels lined up accurately. Drill and screw on each hinge securely. ❏

PATTERNS

Use these patterns to transfer the designs onto your screen. Trace patterns onto tracing paper then using transfer paper, transfer to canvas. If patterns are not actual size, then the percentage of enlargement or reduction is marked. Either reduce or enlarge on a copy machine and transfer to canvas.

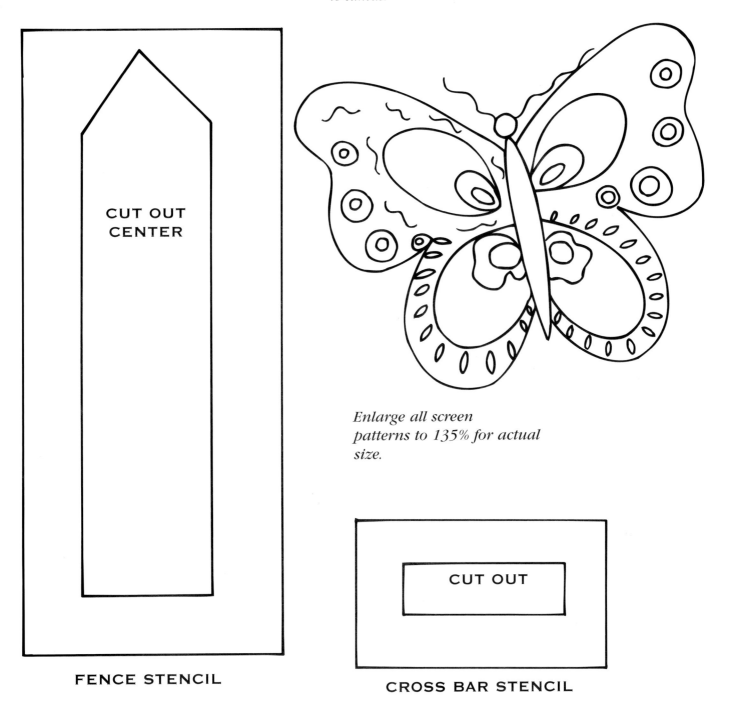

CUT OUT
CENTER

Enlarge all screen patterns to 135% for actual size.

CUT OUT

FENCE STENCIL

CROSS BAR STENCIL

ZINNIA

SMALL YELLOW DAISY

MEDIUM
DAISY

LARGE PINK
DAISY

PATTERNS

Use these patterns to transfer the designs onto your screen. Trace patterns onto tracing paper then using transfer paper, transfer to canvas. If patterns are not actual size, then the percentage of enlargement or reduction is marked. Either reduce or enlarge on a copy machine and transfer to canvas.

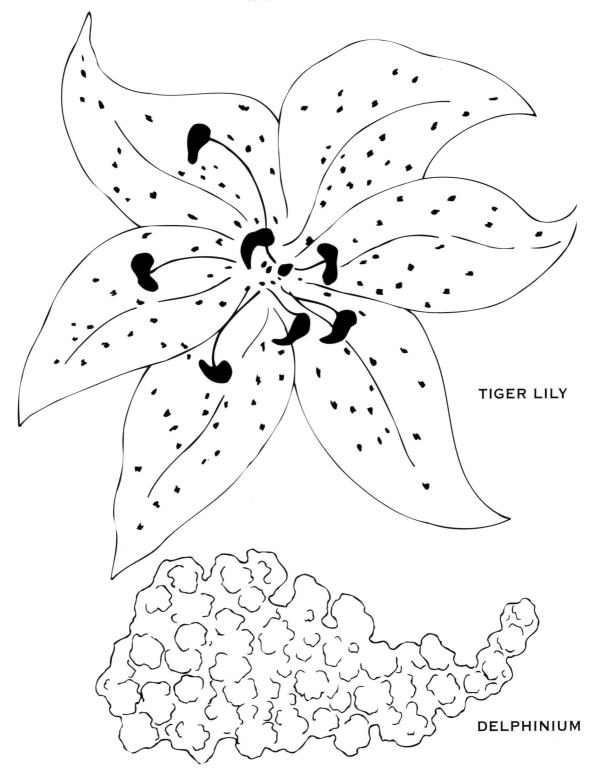

TIGER LILY

DELPHINIUM

Garden
Mural

by Kathi Malarchuk Bailey

A small garden area in the city can become a vast country meadow with a far-reaching view. Just add a fence and extend your garden with a mural. This project is an example. The tree and low partial brick wall bedecked with flowers are part of your garden, while you feel as if you could walk beyond them for miles. If your neighbor's yard interrupts your solitude, this fence can provide a solution for that situation, as well, as you sit and gaze across the meadow and lake to the distant mountains.

See page 116 for Instructions

Continued from page 114

MATERIALS

Fence:
Pre-treated wood fence

Outdoor Paint:
Black
Bright yellow
Dark brown
Dark green
Dark red
Light blue (enough to paint half the fence)
Light green (enough to paint half the fence)
Medium blue
Medium green
Mustard yellow
Off-white
Purple
Terra-cotta
White

Brushes:
Flat paint brush — size 3"
Round artist's brush — size #8
Stencil brushes

Other Supplies:
Stencils of bricks, tulips, hydrangea, and magnolia
    blossom (available in craft stores)
Paint roller
Charcoal pencil
Sea sponges
Masking tape
Measuring tape
Paper palette (available at craft stores, or use
    disposable plates)

INSTRUCTIONS

A diagram of the fence design is given with measurements so that you can see the general scale and proportions of the design — it is not meant to be an actual pattern for the design. It will give you a idea of where to place the horizon, etc. Imagine a serene scene and try your hand at sketching it onto a portion of your fence. Using some of the techniques given here, you will be surprised at what a great mural artist you are.

1. **Sky & Ground:** With paint roller, basecoat top half of fence with light blue (sky) and bottom half with light green (ground). Let dry.

2. Dampen 3" paint brush, dip in purple blended with white, and lightly stroke over sky area for shading.

3. **Clouds:** Sponge clouds with dampened sea sponge and white. Refer to photo of project. Sponge shading to clouds with red blended with white.

4. **Mountains:** Use dampened 3" paint brush to paint mountains at horizon line with light green and medium green (refer to photo of project). Shade with brown.

5. **Lake:** Use dampened 3" brush to paint lake at horizon line with medium blue. Brush lightly with purple blended for white for color variety and shading. Highlight with white.

6. **Meadow:** Use dampened 3" brush and shade green meadow area with brown.

7. **Tree:** Use dampened 3" brush to paint tree trunk and large branches at left with brown (refer to photo for placement). Shade with black and highlight with white, using round brush.

8. **Brick Wall:** Measure up approximately 30" from right bottom — enough for 10-12 rows of bricks — and slant down to the left (see photo of project for brick area). Mask off brick area with tape to protect surrounding areas and basecoat it with off-white. Wipe this area lightly with brown using a sponge. This will be the background grout area for the bricks. Remove tape and let dry.

9. Place brick stencil at lower right corner and adhere with tape. Sponge brick in open area of stencil with dark red. Add sponged touches of color for highlight and shading of mustard yellow, terra-cotta, and black. Remove and reposition stencil and stencil next brick in the same manner. Work in rows across to the left, then upward. Stagger bricks on each row like real bricking.

10. **Hydrangeas:** Stencil hydrangeas above the brick wall so that they appear to be behind the wall. Use medium and dark green for leaves. For blossoms, use medium blue, purple, off-white, and terra-cotta. Use terra-cotta for stems. Stencil some leaves and flowers over top area of the brick wall. Also mask off the top of the brick wall so that some leaves and flowers appear to be partially behind the wall.

11. **Yellow Tulips:** Mask off top of bricks along slanted side for tulip stenciling. Refer to photo for positioning, and stencil tulips leaves and stems with medium and dark green. Stencil blossoms with yellow, shaded with red.

12. **Red Tulips:** Mask off side of tree trunk, and stencil other tulips with red and purple, using photo for reference.

13. **Magnolia:** Stencil magnolia on branches. Stencil blossoms with off-white and shade with brown. Stencil leaves with medium green and dark green. Stencil stems with brown. Add single leaves randomly from the branches. Paint small branches with brown, using the round brush (refer to photo).

14. **Background Foliage and Flowers:** Fill in background with trees and flowers stippled with stencil brushes. Use medium green, yellow, dark green, purple, blue, and brown, referring to photo for color placement. ❑

Ivy Privacy
STAMPED WOODEN FENCE

by Kathi Malarchuk Bailey

MATERIALS

Fence:
Pine Fence, 6 ft. high

Paint:
Exterior latex paint, white (for basecoating fence)
Colored glaze, deep woods green, ivy green, new leaf green, bark brown (found in craft shops where stamping or block printing materials are found)

Brushes:
Sponge brush
Flat artist's brush
#5 round brush

Other Supplies:
Foam design stamps of leaf variety, our has two different size leaves (available at craft stores)
Paper palette (available at craft stores, or use disposable plate)
Sandpaper
Paint roller

Optional for hanging pots:
Wrought iron flower pot holds
Wood screws
Screwdriver
Outdoor sealer

INSTRUCTIONS

1. **Prepare Wood:** Sand wood if necessary. Wipe away dust. Use paint roller to apply one thin coat of paint to fence using white exterior latex paint. Allow to dry then sand lightly. This will create a washed and worn look to fence. Just one coat of paint is absorbed into the wood and makes it look more like a stain.

2. **Stamp Design:** Use a pencil to lightly draw a line to represent a vine climbing along the fence. Use a flat brush to load the glaze paint onto the stamps. Stamp the leaves along the vining line in a variety of colors using the three green colors. Stamps can be loaded with one color, or several colors can be loaded onto the stamp at one time to give variations in the resulting color. Use bark brown, ivy green glaze, and the round brush to add branches and stems.

3. **Finish:** Allow paint to dry for 48 hours. Brush or spray on an outdoor sealer according to general instructions for the product. Attach pot holders to fence if desired. ❏

Retro Flowers

PAINTED WOODEN FENCE

by Kathi Malarchuk Bailey

Want a vegetable garden in part of your yard but you don't want it to spoil the atmosphere of your sitting area or flower garden? Then add a decorative fence between them. There may also be other type areas with different functions that you want to separate. You may have an area with play equipment for children or grandchildren that you want to separate from your flower garden (especially so the flowers don't get trampled.) This happy fence is a wonderful design for designating such an area. It's a particularly easy design to create and will add cheer to any yard, whatever its purpose.

MATERIALS

Fence:
Pre-treated wood fence
Outdoor Paint:
Black
Dark blue
Maroon
Medium blue
Mustard yellow
White
Brushes:
Flat artist's brush — size #10
Round artist's brush — size #8
Sponge brushes
Other Supplies:
Masking tape
Paper palette (available at craft stores, or use paper plate)

INSTRUCTIONS

1. Mask off adjacent panels of fence with tape to protect them from paint as you paint each color. Use tape only on unpainted areas or on completely dry painted areas. After painting, remove tape and reposition it to protect next area. Paint alternate panels with white, medium blue, dark blue, and mustard yellow as shown in photo of project. Let dry.

2. Transfer flower and bee patterns to fence.

3. Paint flowers scattered over fence with maroon and white. (Be sure white flowers are not on white parts of fence.) With the round brush, paint a white swirl design in centers of maroon flowers (refer to photo); paint a dark blue swirl design in centers of white flowers.

4. Paint bee bodies with mustard yellow and black stripes and black heads with white eyes. Paint wings with white and shade with light blue. ❑

Instructions on page 120

PATTERNS

Use these patterns to transfer the designs onto your fence. Trace patterns onto tracing paper then using transfer paper, transfer to wood.

Instructions on page 124

PATTERNS

Use these patterns to transfer the designs onto your fence. Trace patterns onto tracing paper then using transfer paper, transfer to wood.

Enlarge 215% for actual size

Rainbow's End

PAINTED WOOD FENCE

by Kathi Malarchuk Bailey

This fence would be great to get the kids involved with painting. The rainbow is easy to draw and paint and the kids will love being part of this project. This fence would be a welcome design to paint on the fence near a child's play yard. The colorful rainbow plus a pot of sunflowers at its end will inspire happy thoughts. This is an easy and quick design to paint, and it will brighten your view, your day, and your spirits.

MATERIALS

Fence:
Pre-treated wood fence

Outdoor Paint:
Black
Blue
Brown
Green
Indigo
Light blue (enough to paint entire fence)
Orange
Red
Violet
White
Yellow

Brushes:
Flat paint brush — size 3"
Flat artist's brush — size #8
Round artist's brush — size #8

Other Supplies:
Charcoal pencil
Paint roller
Sea sponge
Paper palette (available at craft stores, or use paper plates)

INSTRUCTIONS

1. Basecoat entire fence with light blue, using paint roller. Let dry.

2. Dampen sea sponge and dip it in a small amount of white paint. Sponge clouds on background. Refer to photo of project for placement.

3. With charcoal pencil, lightly outline arc for rainbow. Create rainbow by painting one stroke each of violet, indigo, green, red, orange, and yellow, in that order top to bottom, using the 3" flat paint brush. Blend between colors. Let dry.

4. Transfer pattern of flower pot and sunflowers to fence at the bottom of the rainbow.

5. Paint flower pot with brown and shade with black. Let dry.

6. Paint sunflower centers with brown, using flat artist's brush. Paint petals with yellow, using round brush. Shade petals with orange and highlight with white. Paint leaves and stems with green, using flat artist's brush, and highlight them with yellow. ❑

Metric Conversion Chart

Inches to Millimeters and Centimeters

Inches	MM	CM
1/8	3	.3
1/4	6	.6
3/8	10	1.0
1/2	13	1.3
5/8	16	1.6
3/4	19	1.9
7/8	22	2.2
1	25	2.5
1-1/4	32	3.2
1-1/2	38	3.8
1-3/4	44	4.4
2	51	5.1
3	76	7.6
4	102	10.2
5	127	12.7
6	152	15.2
7	178	17.8
8	203	20.3
9	229	22.9
10	254	25.4
11	279	27.9
12	305	30.5

Yards to Meters

Yards	Meters
1/8	.11
1/4	.23
3/8	.34
1/2	.46
5/8	.57
3/4	.69
7/8	.80
1	.91
2	1.83
3	2.74
4	3.66
5	4.57
6	5.49
7	6.40
8	7.32
9	8.23
10	9.14

INDEX

INDEX